GET TOOLED UP WITH THE STONE AGE SENTINEL

IT'S A MAMMOTH READ!

Cavemates!

Ed Zog here with four million years' worth of history, all crammed into a rock-melting 32 pages!

This here is the STONE AGE SENTINEL, and it's translated from the original Caveman for your comfort and convenience.

HOT

So what have we got? First of all we've got 18 pages of the hottest news this side of an erupting volcano. We start with

the first hominids to walk on two legs rather than four. (What's a hominid? You are, bone brain, and so are any of your ape-man predecessors!)

SWEAT

Read on and find out why bigger brains are best, why sweating is no bad thing, and why fire is the greatest thing since sliced mammoth.

Officially the Stone Age lasts from around 2,000,000 to 2,000 BC. But as we cover much more – from 4,000,000 to 2,000 BC – you're getting more years for your money than any other comparable newspaper!!!

WHAT'S THE CATCH?

And that's not all.

Want to know how to catch a mate Stone Age style?

Curious about what's cooking in the Stone Age stockpot?

Itching to find out what gets them grooving on the Stone Age dance floor?

Read our features between pages 20 and 32!

And remember, if it ain't stone, it ain't worth a bone!!!

Your pal

ed zog

Ed Zog, Editor,
Stone Age Sentinel

ARE YOU A MA OR A MOUSE?

Want to know where you come from? Look at the *Sentinel*'s easy-to-follow family tree and you'll see in a second how you fit into the evolutionary scheme of things...

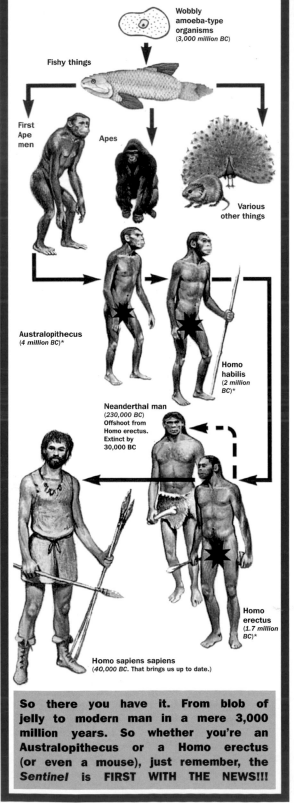

Wobbly amoeba-type organisms (3,000 million BC)

Fishy things

First Ape men

Apes

Various other things

Australopithecus (4 million BC)*

Homo habilis (2 million BC)*

Neanderthal man (230,000 BC) Offshoot from Homo erectus. Extinct by 30,000 BC

Homo erectus (1.7 million BC)*

Homo sapiens sapiens (40,000 BC. That brings us up to date.)

So there you have it. From blob of jelly to modern man in a mere 3,000 million years. So whether you're an Australopithecus or a Homo erectus (or even a mouse), just remember, the Sentinel is FIRST WITH THE NEWS!!!

*The Sentinel is a respectable family newspaper and does not approve of nudity in <u>any</u> era.

TWO LEGS BETTER THAN FOUR

Ape–man in "walking" sensation

4,000,000 BC

Is it a shoe or is it a glove? The age-old debate is over, according to evolutionary whiz-kids *Australopithecus*. From now on, say these ape-men, we don't have to go around on all fours. Instead we can walk upright.

FURROW

The brow-furrowing breakthrough came when this bunch of hominids realized the advantages of standing on two feet.

"It makes us nimbler and faster," said a two-legged spokesman. "It also makes us more versatile – we can carry things and run at the same time, for example. But above all, it gives us a very satisfying impression of height. When you walk on two feet you can peer over bushes, gaze manfully into the distance and grab things from high branches. None of this was possible on all fours."

THICK

"Naturally we will retain some of our earlier characteristics – thick brows, massive jaws, long, strong arms, a tendency to stoop, and awkward table manners – but these will iron themselves out with the passage of time."

Standing a full 1.4m (4½ft) high, and weighing in at 27kg (60lb), *Australopithecus* (or "New Ape-Man") is more than able to cope with the demands of his environment.

Some *Australopithecuses* show off their two-legged skills. "They'll be dancing *Swan Lake* next," sneer rival species.

REELING

Apes who still walk on all four limbs are seriously worried for their future. "It's left us reeling!" said a representative of all-fours pressure group 'Can't Stand Won't Stand.' "There we were minding our own business, when these lanky streaks came darting past on two legs. It spoiled our day.

"We've tried copying them, but we just can't get the hang of it. They say it's like riding a bicycle: once you've learned, you never forget. What nonsense! And what's a bicycle anyway? Take it from me: two legs is downright unnatural!"

Our Getting-Around Correspondent, Larry Plunck says: "Walking is just the tip of the iceberg. Very soon we'll be able to amble, stroll, tiptoe, skip, march and dance the gavotte. The possibilities are endless."

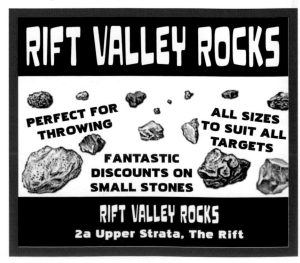

ROCK ON!
IT'S THE STONE AGE!

Homo habilis invents the ancestor of the variable-speed power drill.

THUMBS-UP TOOL TRICK GIVES HUMANS A HELPING HAND

2,000,000 BC

Watch out! There's a new idea about! That's the buzz around the African grassland as *Homo habilis*, the first recognizable human, saunters forth with his amazing new invention – the tool!

"Ever since we realized we didn't have to walk on our hands, we've been wondering what to do with our 'front feet'," a *Homo habilis* told us. "At last we've found the answer. After much experimentation, we discovered that the twiddly parts at the end – now known as fingers – are not only great for picking berries and noses, but can also be used to make tools!"

Tools? We asked top handyman Reggie Lugg to explain.

"Well, you see, a tool is something that does something better than hands – like scissors, dental floss and variable-speed drills with hammer-action for solid walls. Of course, we haven't invented these things yet, but we've made a respectable start by chipping stones to give them a sharp edge. On their own, sharp stones make very good knives. But tie a piece of wood onto them and you've got an axe, or even a spear!"

HACKING

Habilis means "skilled", and there's no doubt that *Homo habilis* is living up to his name. He's chipping and hacking like there's no tomorrow. In fact, he looks set to take over the whole world!

Ape-man *Australopithecus* is resigned to extinction. But they've got a few points to raise before they go.

"These new hominids may be clever, but they're a messy bunch," said one ape-person. "They leave their little shards of sharpened stone lying all over the place. What if our kids cut themselves on one of these things? We've still got another 800,000 years to go before we die out, so we think they ought to be more considerate. I'll bet people will still be picking up their mess millions of years from now."

Pleased to meat you!

HUNTER-GATHERERS COME OUT TOP AS MEAT MANIA SWEEPS GLOBE

2,000,000 BC

It's Pick 'n' Mix time for us hominids as we face up to a brand new menu. Until now, we've had to content ourselves with picking berries, roots and the odd vegetable. Thanks to *Homo habilis*, however, a new item has been added to the menu – meat!

RUM

"Blearggh! Can't stand the stuff! Give me a nice rummage in the shrubs," said top *Australopithecus* ape-man and vegetarian, Ronnie Lurch.

But veggies like Lurch are up against stiff competition. Almost every kind of animal, from a gazelle to a quagga*, can find green stuff and eat it quicker than ape-men can. The only way to survive is to eat meat as well as veg.

GO FORTH

"It's all very well saying to go forth and gather," said leading *Homo habilis* Cornelius Gogg. "But in today's competitive environment you need to hunt too. That's why we're carving a niche for ourselves as hunter-gatherers."

The new breed of hunter-gatherers have set themselves a strict agenda. They've got a month in each area to strip all available vegetation, kill whatever they can, and then move on to new ground.

Ape-men have responded with a detailed manifesto called 'Veg Is Best'. But their pledge that 'Brussels Sprouts Taste Nice' has been greeted with widespread derision.

* Modern-day hunter-gatherers please note: a quagga is a washed-out zebra which disappeared around AD 1900, so don't bother looking for it now.

This stuff is packed full of protein and is very tasty! It's more difficult to catch than a plant, but experts say it's definitely worth the extra effort.

3

Here we go, here we go! A bunch of burly hominids flex those all-important brain muscles.

THINK BIG

SIZE MATTERS, SAY BRAIN GURUS

2,000,000 BC

A brain may not appear as immediately useful as a good set of teeth," head expert Professor Elmer Yarg said yesterday, "but it's indispensable if you want to get ahead in life. And research has shown that the bigger it is, the better you'll do."

LACK

Prof. Yarg and his colleagues claim that big brains make up for our lack of fangs, talons, tusks, claws, poison glands and other frightening things.

"If you have a big brain, you can outwit creatures with smaller brains," said Prof. Yarg. "It's that simple. And as humans have got the biggest brains in the world, we can outwit anything.

"Physically, we're weak and vulnerable. But we've got it up top and that's what counts. I wouldn't be surprised if we became the leading creatures on the planet."

AHEM

Opponents have slammed the big-brain theory on the grounds that human females' birth canals are not big enough to deliver children with big brains.

Prof. Yarg has the answer. "It's very straightforward. What happens is that we're born with small brains and then they increase in size as we grow older. Other species do this, but they don't do it as well as we do. A human baby's brain is 25% of what it will be in adulthood. A chimpanzee, by comparison, is born with 65% of its total brain power."

(Adult human brains are almost twice as big as a chimpanzee's, and by the 20th century AD they'll be three times as big. Wow!)

"Granted, there are some drawbacks. While the baby's brain is growing, it's completely dependent on its parents. A baboon can look after itself after 12 months, whereas it takes a good six years for human kids to get the hang of things. So that means an awful lot more time and effort for the parents."

BRAIN OR BRAWN?

Decide for yourself which is best with our handy check list!

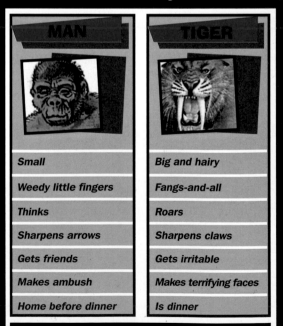

MAN	TIGER
Small	*Big and hairy*
Weedy little fingers	*Fangs-and-all*
Thinks	*Roars*
Sharpens arrows	*Sharpens claws*
Gets friends	*Gets irritable*
Makes ambush	*Makes terrifying faces*
Home before dinner	*Is dinner*

HERE AT THE SENTINEL WE SAY THERE'S NO CONTEST!!! IT LOOKS LIKE THE BRAIN IS THE DEADLIEST WEAPON OF ALL.

PERSPIRATION? NO SWEAT!

MAN CHILLS OUT

2,000,000 BC

Do your smelly armpits embarrass you? Well don't you worry. According to the latest evidence, sweating buckets is a major bonus.

Dr. Oscar Snig explains all:

"Living as we do in Africa, it is vital to be able to keep cool. The basic way of doing this for most species is to lie in the shade, put out your tongue and pant. But this makes you look silly and is only effective in short bursts. If you do it on the run, you get dizzy and fall over – not to mention finding your mouth full of flies. That's why all the big predators tend not to do much round about midday."

LYING IN THE SUN

"Humans can't afford to lie around, especially at midday when the pickings'll be good, since the other carnivores are out of the way. So we've come up with two classy ways of keeping cool AND being able to hunt at the same time. First of all, we've lost most of our body hair. And secondly, we've learned how to sweat.

"Sweating is an incredibly efficient form of temperature control. The moment you get too hot, your body oozes water which cools you by evaporation. This means you can chase those pesky gazelles without having to stop every few minutes for a pant."

EXCESS

However, Snig warns, excess perspiration can be dangerous. Humans can only tolerate water loss amounting to 10% of their total body weight. Overly-enthusiastic sweaters run the risk of becoming dehydrated.

"It's very important to replace lost fluid. Some animals can store water very effectively – a camel, for example, can take aboard about 20 buckets of water in 10 minutes. Humans can only store a hundredth of that in the same time. Therefore, I'd advise people to sweat only in areas where there are plenty of rivers and streams."

SENTINEL VERDICT:

Smell bad. It's the way forward. And you can forget about unsightly sweat stains because we don't wear clothes.

Dr. Snig's book *Why We're Not Camels* comes out in August. RRP 15.99 pebbles.

NEXT WEEK: ARE HICCUPS A HELP?

A hominid doing some sweating. Unfortunately for his chums, it'll be two million years before someone invents the underarm deodorant.

"THEY WERE SMALL AND STUPID"

NEW GENERATION TRASHES 'SKILLED' BREED

1,700,000 BC

The latest race of humans has a r r i v e d ! They're big, they're brainy, they're the best – they're *Homo erectus!*

The new kids on the block take a dim view of their ancestors, *Homo habilis*, whom they brand as "stunted dimwits."

"They may have been clever for their time," said Al 'Upright' Ugg, "but compared to us, they're nothing. We're a good 50cm (20in) taller, we're over 20kg (44lbs) heavier, and as for our brains – well, let's just say you can think a whole lot better with an extra whole 15% of the grey crinkly stuff."

TOOLS

With their greater size and their advanced tool-making capabilities, *Homo erectus* are certainly making their mark on the evolutionary scene. But some of them are asking the question, 'How come we're so big?'

Homo habilis – Yesterday's man

"Easy," said Al. "Big animals need less energy, relative to their body weight, than small animals. Marmosets, for example, eat proportionally three times as much as a human. So if food is scarce, it's actually more efficient to be big. Still confused? Never mind. You've got plenty of time to figure it out because we're going to be here for the next 1.5 million years!"

FIRE IN THE HOLE

Bright Sparks Cause Flame Sensation

Fire. Once you've tamed it you can't live without it, and it has so many uses. These hungry hominids are using it to confuse and frighten their dinner.

450,000 BC

It's hot, it makes you sweat and it's not curry. Yes, it's FIRE!

Previously considered somewhat frightening, the amazing red stuff has become man's best friend. All over the world, humans are using it to cook, to keep warm and to frighten wild beasts.

STRIKES

"There's nothing new about fire," said Norris Nik, President of the Hearth Trust. "You can find it all over the place – bush fires, lightning strikes and volcanoes, for example. But the breakthrough has been introducing it to the home. What you do is make a little pile of stuff, then you find your nearest source of fire, stick a long piece of wood into it and hurry back to light your stuff. If the stuff doesn't burn – and if it's stone or earth it probably won't – try a pile of different stuff. It sounds complicated, but it's very simple really."

LOTS

Fire has lots of things going for it, the main one being that it gives us humans more control of our surroundings.

"Before, we depended on the Sun for heat and light," enthused Norris. "Now we can keep warm and dry wherever we are. This not only spells an end to dank caves but it means we can survive in cold places like Europe. And if any Ice Age comes along we can just sit it out."

GROOMING

Scientists aren't sure what fire is, but the current opinion is that it may be some kind of animal.

"In its natural state, fire can be extremely dangerous. However, it is easily tamed and makes a perfect household pet. It's easy to look after, requiring no grooming or vet's visits, and survives happily on a diet of twigs and dry grass. But it does tend to die if given too much to drink.

"Its only drawback is that it leaves nasty stains on the ceiling – but if you have bats already you'll be used to that."

WHAT A DUMP!

Europe a "cultural wasteland"

478,000 BC

Paris in the springtime? Swinging London? Rome, the eternal city? Pah! Give us a break!

Are we disappointed or what? Having trudged all the way to Europe, we've found it's got no croissants, no fancy pasta shapes, no cute little cities, no castles and no scandal-prone royal families. In fact, it has a noticeable lack of anything interesting at all.

SHIVER

"It's a cold, miserable place with a lot of mountains, forests and rivers," said shivering Debby Klunk, one of the first wave of settlers. "In the north it's nothing but snow and ice. If we stay here long enough I wouldn't be at all surprised if we ended up with pale skins, an embarrassing amount of body hair and a deplorable sense of rhythm. We should never have left Africa."

BAD

However, sources reveal that Europe isn't as bad as it's made out to be. For starters, it's a lot drier than Africa. Moreover, it's got an abundance of animals and is therefore a tip-top destination for hunters.

As numbers grow in the African grasslands and humans begin to feel the pinch, we say: "Go North young man!"

LET'S STEPPE ON IT!

MAN GETS INTO THE ASIAN SWING

400,000 BC

"Europe? Why go there?" asks laid-back hominid Hussein Ogg, basking outside his Asian cave. "That's a place for stupid people."

Hussein has a point. Besides being cold and nasty, Europe is also very small. Asia, on the other hand, is mostly warm, is crammed with herds of wildlife, has millions of acres of grassland, and stretches from the Mediterranean to the Pacific.

TOP TRIP

According to a recent hunter-gatherer survey, Asia is our No. 1 destination. Visitors enjoy:
- Nice climate
- Open spaces
- Plenty of food
- The opportunity to become Chinese and invent practically everything before anybody else does.

ENDLESS

Particular attention has been focused on three main rivers – the

Life in a cave, somewhere in Asia. These people could even be heading for China!

Euphrates in Mesopotamia, the Yellow in China and the Indus in India.

"Asia has endless potential," said migration rep. Sally-Sue Grunk. "But it's the big river systems that seem to be the main draw. People say conditions are very comfortable there and, given enough time, they might even settle down and start farming."

THERE'S NO PLACE LIKE HOME!

By Sentinel correspondent KEN ZOG

Cave shortage prompts hut-building spree

380,000 BC

The world is echoing to the sound of wolf whistles as humans hitch up their furs, dust off their tasteless jokes and get into some serious construction work.

Building has become big business thanks to the pressures of growing populations and an increasing shortage of accommodation.

JUST

"There just aren't enough caves to go round," said Len Mukk (building, decorating and allied trades). "People are coming up and saying, 'Len, knock me up a hut will you? Nothing fancy – just enough space for me and the wife, with somewhere to stick the rest of the family.' So I tell 'em it'll take two weeks and we go from there – strictly pebbles-in-hand, mind you. You can't give credit in today's economic climate."

FLIMSY

Len and his mates are particularly busy in Europe, where decent

"Pah, who did your drains? It'll cost you to have them done properly," say builders.

caves are rare outside of southern France.

"Now and then a customer complains that his home's too flimsy. So I say, 'Look son. You're a hunter-gatherer. You're on the move all the time. You don't want nothing permanent. I've built you a nice little one-room hut out of leafy branches. You've got a row of central posts and some stonework around the edges so's it doesn't blow away. There's a hearth in the middle and space for you all to huddle down in your furs at night. It'll last you the season. Then you'll be moving on. What more do you want? If you're after the Palace of Versailles you should have said so.' There's no reasoning with some, is there?"

HIPPOS IN THE THAMES?

PALM TREES IN GREENLAND?

What's going on?

Where the ice goes when there's an Ice Age. (Just in case you're interested...)

Glaciers

An Investigative Special Report by Olsen Mug*

130,000 BC

Weather! Can't live with it, can't live without it. One millennium you're shivering in your furs, and the next you're squabbling over who gets the suntan lotion first. Hot, cold, hot, cold – it's enough to make you dizzy.

Our unpredictable climate has been a source of irritation for hundreds of thousands of years. But thanks to a special investigation by *Sentinel* super-sleuth, Olsen Mug*, we now know why it acts like it does.

LIES

"The secret lies in the way the Earth goes around the Sun," says Olsen Mug*. "Its orbit isn't always the same. Sometimes it takes us farther away from the Sun, and sometimes it takes us closer.

"This means that we have successive Ice Ages, with glaciers reaching as far south as London and New York, followed by ice-free periods when the earth is warm and fertile, lions wander through Europe, and Britons shelter beneath palm trees, and have to plaster on Factor 20 mud when they sunbathe."

TRAP

"This also explains the puzzling phenomenon of why, at times, land is sometimes above the sea and sometimes beneath it. When it's cold, most of the world's water is trapped in glaciers and sea levels are low. But when it gets hot, the glaciers melt and we have lots of rain, therefore sea levels rise."

AWKWARD

"Of course, all this toing and froing does have its awkward moments.

"Imagine you're a hippo, wallowing in the Thames. Then along comes an Ice Age and everybody starts pointing and acting like you don't belong. How embarrassing! And then you have other problems, like not being able to survive because it's too cold, and all the plants you usually eat don't grow where you live anymore. It does make life difficult."

SPELL

How long can we expect this to continue? "Almost indefinitely," says Olsen Mug*. "A prolonged warm spell is predicted from about 13,000 BC, but things will start cooling off around the 21st century AD.

"Maybe by then, though, they'll have discovered the secret of global warming."

IT'S A KNOCKOUT!

100,000 BC

Wise man wins human race

The name's Sap – Hom double sap." Yes, it's hands up to *Homo sapiens sapiens*, the hominid who's licensed to kill.

Despite stiff competition, *Hom. sap. sap.* – "the wisest of the wise" – has won through to become the top species on Earth.

"It's all to do with being extremely clever," one *Homo sapiens sapiens* admitted modestly. "With our advanced skills, we are in every way superior to any other type of being."

TOOLS

It is all true. *Homo sapiens sapiens* has the most powerful brain of any hominid. And with this massive amount of grey stuff, they have been able to create increasingly complex tools and, above all, develop a sophisticated language. (You can read more about this on pages 24-25, word fans.)

WEIGHT LOSS

It doesn't matter that *Hom. sap. sap.* is only two-thirds the weight of predecessor *Homo erectus*. Being able to speak properly means they can plan, exchange ideas and generally stir things up to their own benefit.

"We may be less bulky than previous species, but we have evolved THE definitive brain size," says Dr. Heinrich Zag, an expert in his field. "There will be no comparable brain for the foreseeable future. People in 2000 AD may look back and say, 'Oh how uncivilized they were!' But the fact is, our brains and bodies are exactly the same as those hominids on the 7:30am train from Richmond."

OLSEN MUG
Special Reporter

G'DAY!

CAVEMATES DISCOVER AUSTRALIA!

50,000 BC

First it was Europe, then it was Asia. Now humankind has taken over God's own garden, the land of the roo and the billabong – Australia!

UNDERSIDE

"Strewth, it's peculiar out here, mate," said Bob Awk, one of the first settlers. "The place is hot as a billycan's underside for starters. And the wildlife – well, either someone's playing a joke or they've been left to evolve on their own for too long. Take the kangaroo – big feller, bounds along on its hind legs and carries its kids in a little pouch. Believe me, you don't find that kind of creature anywhere else in the world. Same goes for the wallaby, the koala, the kookaburra and the duck-billed platypus. Queer as a three-dollar bill, the lot of 'em. And as for the XXXXXXX flies...

"Still, the surfing's good and there's some impressive deserts we can go walkabout in. Could be worse."

GATHER

Australia may be special, but it's not half as special as the way it was colonized. From what our reporters can gather, a huge number of *Homo sapiens sapiens* in Indonesia simply got in their boats and said, "Let's go to Australia." And off they went!

That's pretty amazing, especially when our fortune-tellers predict that it'll be another 51,788 years before anybody else realizes Australia exists.

And, they say, guess what the new bunch of *Hom. sap. saps.* will call the old bunch of *Hom. sap. saps.* when they find them in the 18th century AD? Aborigines! That's from the Latin "*Ab Origine*" which means "From the beginning."

"Well," says Bob, "if we're from the beginning, does that mean they're the end? Future hominids should give that a bit of thought!"

Bob Awk and cavemate go in search of Australia's weird and wonderful wildlife.

"DEAD END" SHOCK
FOR ALTERNATIVES
NEANDERTHALS TOLD "YOU'RE NOBODIES"

40,000 BC

Neanderthals have been doing their best to become an alternative race of humans. But their hopes were quashed at a recent convention of hominids when it was revealed that they lacked all the major qualifications.

DEVASTATED

"I'm devastated!" said beetle-browed Grr Ngg. "We seriously thought we were going places. But as the convention wore on, we realized that we were way behind the competition!"

When the low-slung, chunky Neanderthals first appeared in about 230,000 BC, their prospects were as good as anybody else's. True, they looked a bit brutish and ape-like, but they were pretty sophisticated. They cared for their old and sick, they developed a primitive religion and buried their dead with flowers and gifts – though some experts have dismissed this as "mere corpse disposal".

YAK

"It was "Hom-oh-so-high-and-mighty" sapiens sapiens who spelled our downfall," said Grr. "We couldn't match his tool-making skills and we simply couldn't understand what he was yakking on about. That was our big failing – speech. Hom. sap. sap. can say things like 'Hello gorgeous, how about a date?' All we can do is grunt a bit and make vivid hand signals. We're washed up. By 30,000 BC we won't be here and everyone will say 'Where have those interesting alternative type humans gone?'"

LOST LORE OF THE NEANDERTHALS

No. 1 of our occasional series brings you the secrets of Neanderthal etiquette

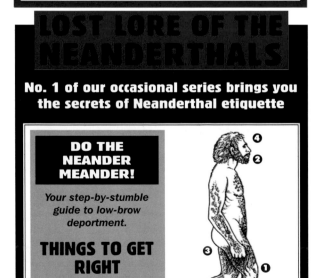

DO THE NEANDER MEANDER!

Your step-by-stumble guide to low-brow deportment.

THINGS TO GET RIGHT

1. Knees bent
2. Chin out
3. Fists curled
4. Brow furrowed

LET'S COME TOGETHER!
GOOD VIBES FOR TRIBES

Being in a big group of fellow hominids is much more fun than mooching around on your own, even if you do end up seeing far more of Uncle Zog than you'd care to.

30,000 BC

It's true – solitary scavenging can damage your health! According to reports, you're likely to wither and die unless you're part of a tribe.

Communal living has been the rage for some time now. It started way back when early hominids stood upright and had to care for their children. This led to...

1. Small groups of hominids sticking together.

Then there came the business of hunting which, in order to be successful, required...

2. Cooperation with other groups.

After that came language, and as everyone knows, if you speak, you need someone to speak to, so that led to...

3. Gossip, general chit-chat and telling Waffly Zog to shut up on the mammoth hunt.

Then came the pressures of migrating to different places, facing ferocious foreign beasts and checking the toilet for poisonous spiders. This encouraged us to...

4. Group together in the face of adversity in even greater numbers.

And so we formed tribes!

BAND

What's a tribe? Simple. We tend to hunt and gather in groups of 30 or so (12 adults and their kids). When 20 of these groups get together they form a band of around 600. This is a tribe. We meet for big hunts, the odd ceremony and all sorts of other things – like making up new words, exchanging ideas, and most important of all, pairing up and having lots of little hominids.

So, at the end of the day, whether you're in Cairo or Cambridge, you're definitely safer with a tribe!

CAVE DWELLERS IN GRAFFITI UPROAR

"BUT IS IT ART?" SAY CRITICS

15,000 BC

French cave dwellers from Lascaux, in the Dordogne, are hopping mad. They've been branded as "destructive lay-abouts" – all on account of a little wall painting.

"They're vandals," said Lascaux local Mme. Bovary D'Ag. "Before these people moved in, the caves were in excellent condition. Now they're covered in graffiti which will cost a great deal to remove. They call it art. But I've seen them at it. They frolic around, daubing half-finished pictures of animals on the wall and then, late at night, some bright spark'll fill his mouth with paint and spray it out to make an outline of his hand. Frankly, they're a menace."

PLIGHT

"Oh, the plight of the struggling artist!" moaned Vincent van Ugh, a cave painter. "These paintings aren't graffiti. They're the first clear sign of man's artistic ability. They prove we can move beyond the day-to-day business of staying alive and can devote ourselves to more complex activity.

"What's more, art is a vital part of our kids' upbringing. Look. Here's a bull. And here's its hoof print. See? During the long winter months, we put a lot of effort into these paintings so that our children can recognize animals and their tracks.

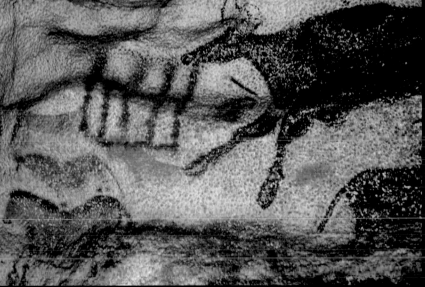
"Cows in French Art". Number one in a series of 100 great cow paintings. Collect the set!

It makes the hunting season so much easier. Imagine what would happen if we didn't do it. We'd have kids rushing at a cave lion shouting, "Gazelle! Easy meat!"

A CHILD OF FIVE COULD DO IT

Locals aren't convinced. "Some of the graffiti is quite unrecognizable as man or beast," says Mme. Bovary. "And look at the roof. It's covered in soot. They must have been lighting fires indoors. We don't need these kind of tenants. They're little better than squatters."

The unappreciated cave artists have agreed to move on. But they refuse to remove either the wall paintings or the layers of broken flints and small bones that cover the floor.

"The landlord wants to keep our deposits? Right. There they are, he can keep them!"

HAND SIGNAL

News has come in that our Stone-Age artists are mostly right-handed. From a sample of 158 hand outlines discovered in the French cave of Gargas, 136 were painted by the right hand and only 22 by the left.

But our art expert warns: "These figures could be misleading. We need to include further data from findings in Germany, Portugal, Italy and Sicily to get a fuller picture of which hand is more commonly used in the European Community."

A report is expected within the next 32,000 years.

THE BUCK
DOESN'T STOP HERE

Stone Age joke: Q. What's the difference between a bat and a bison? A. If you don't know, I certainly won't be asking you to go hunting! (Cue polite laughter.)

LAND OF OPPORTUNITY BECKONS

12,000 BC

It's a whole new continent! Intrepid trekkers in northern Siberia have discovered a land bridge leading from the Eurasian continent to America!

UNPLEASANT

Early reports say America is a cold and unpleasant place with little going for it.

"You'd have to be an Eskimo to survive there," said one disappointed colonist. "It's like living in Alaska."

Land bridge to Alaska

They went thataway!

However, geographical experts have pointed out that the place they've found is, in fact, Alaska, and that a sunnier climate awaits to the south.

Sentinel reporters have followed emigrants on their great trek, and can confirm that America gets hotter the farther down you go.

PASS

"First you pass through this cold area," says cub-reporter Jimmy Olsen-Clod, "then you reach a country of big open spaces and endless opportunity. It's a fantastic place. There's endless prairies with million-strong herds of bison, and fields and fields of things like beans and corn.

"These foods are brand-new to us. But then so are a lot of other things here – turkeys, avocados, guinea-pigs, squashes and an irritating little dog called a Chihuahua."

Jimmy Olsen-Clod predicts that it'll take at least 2,000 years to reach the bottom of the continent.

"There's so much to see and explore. I reckon we won't be in Chile until 10,000 BC at the earliest."

WE'RE GOING TO POT

"Not a copy" say Japanese

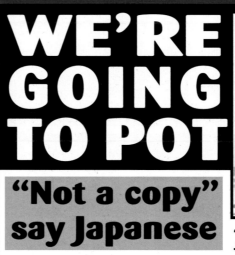

"It's all our own work," insist Japanese potters.

12,000 BC

Japan has invented the most useful piece of pottery to date – the pot.

"It is a major break-through," said Professor Tanaka Stig. "We are now able to construct containers of any type we like simply by shaping lumps of clay and baking them in a covered pit.

"Unfortunately we are not able to use these pots as much as we would like. They are, alas, too heavy and too fragile to fit in with our hunting and gathering existence. Nevertheless, the art of pottery is here to stay and will undoubtedly be useful if people settle down to become farmers."

CLAIM

Opponents are already claiming the invention is a mere copy, and point to the existence of pottery skills in Czechoslovakia as far back as 25,000 BC.

LACKING

However, Professor Stig haughtily dismisses the earlier examples of pottery as "mere statuettes" which are "utterly lacking in usefulness."

"Pottery is a genuine first for Japan," he insists, "and should fill us with justifiable national pride."

MAMMOTH SHORTAGE

CAUSES CONCERN

LIFESTYLE COLLAPSE
PREDICTED FOR MANY

12,000 BC

Residents of eastern Europe and northern Asia are in big trouble. The mammoth, their main source of food, is disappearing FAST.

The mammoth has been a big item for centuries. Hunters have valued it for its legendary size (*Ed. actually, it's slightly smaller than an elephant*), its ivory tusks, its wonderful woolly hide and equally woolly brain.

Mammoths are so stupid and cumbersome that people have had no trouble laying an ambush and picking them off as they plod through the countryside. Sometimes they didn't even have to kill them. Quite often they found dead ones deep frozen and covered in ice and snow. All they had to do then was thaw them out at leisure using the miracle of fire.

SHREW

But all that's in the past. Nowadays, hunters lying in wait on the mammoth trail count themselves lucky if they bag a pygmy shrew.

What's happened? Mrs. Dunk, from the Russian village of Kostienki, tells all: "It's the men! They wouldn't stop killing mammoths. I told them they'd have problems if they carried on, but they took no notice. Now look what's happened. We've run out of the things. What can I do? Mr. Dunk won't touch his tea unless there's a big chunk of mammoth on the plate."

HALF

Experts say Mrs. Dunk is half right. The climate around Kostienki is also changing. It used to be freezing cold, and now it's getting warmer. And as the snow and ice retreats to the north, so the few remaining mammoths are following after it.

"Yes," bellowed a mammoth spokesperson, "we've all got these thick shaggy coats, so we like things nice and cold. This hot weather makes us all sweaty and bad-tempered, so we're following our chums the reindeer to colder climes, where we can bask around in snowdrifts."

This is very bad news for Kostienki, which has taken mammoth-mania to the limits. Not only do its inhabitants eat mammoths, but they even build houses out of them. The doors are made of tusks and the walls are made of various other bones. The whole thing is pinned together with smaller bones, tied up with mammoth sinew and covered with hide.

Bone sweet bone – It's a mammoth house.

The framework alone of a typical mammoth house, 5m (16ft) wide, weighs a staggering 21,000kg (46,000lb)! And some of their houses are much bigger than that!

THERE'S MORE

And what do you do in Kostienki when it's a bit cold? You throw a few mammoth bones on the fire! What do you do if you feel like creating a figurine of old Mrs. Zunk with her big nose? You get out your knife and a chunk of mammoth tusk!

MAD

Tools, toys, houses, food, clothes, furniture, knick-knacks – they're mammoth mad. In the whole village there's hardly a spoon or a needle that didn't start life as part of a mammoth.

So what are the Kostienkians going to do now?

"It's a clear choice," said Mr. Dunk. "We either make do with something else or go north in search of any remaining mammoths."

Bye-bye mammoth, we're missing you already!

Experts say overhunting, a changing environment and having a small brain has finished off the mammoth.

MAMMOTH UPDATE NEXT WEEK

FARMING FRENZY
HITS FERTILE CRESCENT

HUNTER-GATHERERS WARN OF "MUTANT INVASION"

Some new-fangled farmers buckle down to some reaping what they sow, counting their chickens, and not letting one bad apple spoil the whole barrel.

7,500 BC

It's put-your-feet-up time in the Middle East, as folk discover the delights of farming.

Lifestyle experts from the Fertile Crescent ("It's a big lump of land running from Egypt to Iran, including the bottom bit of Turkey," says our Geography Correspondent) have found that folk live much more comfortably if they stop hunting and gathering, and take up farming instead.

SEED

What is farming? We asked a local agri-spokesman: "It's simple. You throw a few handfuls of seed around and wait for it to grow. Then you eat whatever it grows into. In between times you wander about waving a big stick, shouting, 'Get off my land!' It's more exciting than picking berries and it's a whole lot easier than chasing antelopes, I can tell you!"

But hunter-gatherers are lobbying for agriculture to be outlawed. "It's a menace to the natural order and it's putting us out of business," said a representative. "Farmers are selecting mutant plants, which grow bigger than normal. And then they're planting them! It ought to be banned NOW!"

DESTROY

Farmers have laughed off suggestions that agriculture will destroy the countryside. "In the Fertile Crescent we're growing wheat, barley, peas, lentils – the works. It's the up-and-coming thing. India, China and South America will all be at it soon. And I'll tell you why. 15 square km (5.82 square miles) of fields can support 150 farmers. It takes 650 square km (250 square miles) to support 25 hunter-gatherers. Need I say more?"

STAINS

In a further break from tradition, farmers are building villages. These groups of dwellings are made from wood and stone, are usually found near a spring, and are designed to last for several years. Opponents say that villages are only the start and will lead to mega-settlements with inner-city crime and graffiti-stained underpasses.

Hunter-gatherers are planning a "Hunt 'n' Gather" protest march to draw attention to this unpleasant prospect. Their precise route is unknown but they are expected to wander in small, unhappy groups across Africa, Europe and Asia.

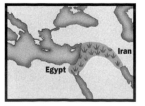

It's fertile and it's a crescent.

A STITCH IN TIME...

FUR FLIES AS FLAX SPARKS CLOTHING CRAZE

7,500 BC

It's official! Those Kill-things-and-wear-'em days are over. From now on it's pelts off and clothes on as the rag trade takes over!

Thanks to an enterprising bunch of farmers, we no longer have to wear furs. Instead we can wear "cloth". This miracle fabric is guaranteed to be light, comfortable, quickly mended and easily replaced.

FLAX FAX

Sentinel reporters have identified the source of "cloth" as a plant called flax. According to informants, raw flax has to be soaked, pounded vigorously and then rubbed on the thigh to make a weavable strand.

"It's hard work," agreed style guru Giovanni Lugg, "But it's worth the trouble. As for furs, they're totally out of fashion – unless you live somewhere really cold. All that hair, and those rubbery fleshy tendrils. Ugh! Take it from me. Cloth's the people's choice."

Fashionable flax takes hours of dedicated work to process into the new miracle material "cloth".

TAME THAT BEAST
DOMESTICATION SENSATION!

Farming isn't just about crops. You'll need tame animals too. Here at the *Sentinel* we've drawn up a handy guide to a happy barnyard. Follow our chart to what stings and bites and what doesn't (or oughtn't to, at any rate) and you'll never go hunting or gathering again.

Aurochs

Stands 1.8m (6ft) at the shoulder. Muscly and bad-tempered. Has big, curved horns. Dislikes red rags. Provides a great deal of meat, leather and milk. Bellows and goes "Moo".

VERDICT – *An unlikely candidate, but since it provides so much, it's worth the trouble. Capture a few, breed from the placid ones and Hey Presto! You've got cows.*

Snake

Comes in all sizes. Slithery. Often poisonous. Impossible to milk. Unreliable egg-layer. Goes "Hiss".

VERDICT – *Don't bother. But keep a few on the refuse tip because they eat rats.*

Sheep and goat

About knee-height. Has horns. Provides warm, thick wool, milk and meat. Goes "Baa" and "Mehh".

VERDICT – *Ideal for the farm. They're herd animals, so once you've caught a few young 'uns, they'll think you're herd leader and will do what you tell 'em (sort of).*

Wild boar

Smaller than sheep. Fat. Bristly. Has tusks and twirly tail. Provides bacon, chops and crackling. Goes "Oink".

VERDICT – *Yummy! Every home should have one. Is intelligent and eats anything, so is a natural for those rundown filth strewn farms. Needs almost no taming. Comes home at night of its own accord. Often called Pig.*

Cat

Small. Plain, striped or tabby. Edible only on TV documentaries about funny foreigners. Goes "Miaouw" and "Browwp". Can scratch when irritated.

VERDICT – *Will accept domestication with a superior shrug. Eats mice, rats, small rabbits and birds and leaves their indigestible parts on your floor. Tends to trip you up but can be kicked very satisfactorily. Likes scratching furniture which is OK so long as your sitting log doesn't evolve into a sofa which you've upholstered at great expense. Comforting lap accessory.*

Believe it or not, over time this thing can be bred into a French poodle! (Would we lie to you?!?)

Tiger

Large, striped, frightening thing. Big teeth. Big appetite. Prone to scenes of explicit violence. Goes "Wraaaaaaagh."

VERDICT – *Only worth keeping if you have a particularly irksome milkman or if you belong to the "I-think pit-bulls-and-Dobermans-are-soft" school of pet lovers. Otherwise forget it. Try its lesser cousin, the cat.*

Fly

Has wings. Small and black. Plenty of eggs but too small to see. Creepy eyes. Spits on food. Tastes through feet. Goes "Buzz".

VERDICT – *Impossible to domesticate. Avoid like the plague.*

Wolf

Small, rangy scavenger. Howls at night. Not worth eating but plays educational role in bedtime stories. Goes "Woof".

VERDICT – *A pack animal, so if you get a puppy it'll follow you around. Will help you out hunting, will fetch your slippers when you come home and will bark all day if you leave it inside.*

WARNING!

Take care not to breed from animals that are too closely related, otherwise THIS could happen, or worse!

AGRICULTURE OR AGRI-VATION?

FARMERS SAY "BAA!" TO ANIMALS

6,500 BC

Farming, which many thought would be a great leap forward for humankind, isn't such a good idea after all.

"We should never have given up hunting and gathering," says farmer Giles Gnug from Jericho, in the Fertile Crescent. "Agriculture is hard work, the diet's less varied, bandits keep stealing our food and we catch all these nasty new diseases."

GERMS

Diseases? Yes. If you live close to animals for too long, you catch viruses from them. The result is that human beings, who've never had a cold in their lives, are now prone to all sorts of deadly things like measles, smallpox and influenza.

"And that's not all," says farmer Giles. "If you live in a village, as most farmers do, surrounded by lots of people and all their filth, that means you're much likelier to catch whatever's going around than if you're hunting and gathering on the plains.

"Dysentery, typhoid, tuberculosis – you name it, we've got it. And some of these villages are in really unhealthy places. I've heard of this farming community at Çatal Hüyük in Turkey, for example, which is surrounded by mosquito infested marshes and everyone catches malaria and dies at an early age. But then it was one of the first settlements, so maybe they didn't know any better."

In fact, most farmers can expect to die before they're 35 – or 30 if they're women.

So why do people do it? "Ah well," says Giles. "The trouble is there's so many of us. Once we started to get a regular supply of food, we bred like rabbits, and now we're stuck with it. If we went back to hunting and gathering we'd all starve. It's too late to change now."

DID YOU KNOW...

• Nothing grows in the Sahara because all the goodness has been washed out of the soil by massive amounts of rainfall.

• The hefty old Aurochs – giant ancestor of the cow – won't be extinct until AD 1671.

• A typical Stone-Age head of corn is only the size of a thumb nail! (This is why we haven't bothered inventing pointy things to stick in the ends of corn-on-the-cob!)

Lost for smalltalk? Read the *Sentinel*!

Sheep. They may look cute and cuddly, but beneath the thin veneer of baaahsome amiability there lies a deadly, malevolent menace to mankind.

HOW IRRIGATING

Water load of old ditches!

3,500 BC

Wouldn't it be nice if we could grow more crops? Well now we can – thanks to irrigation, a cunning method of bringing water to places that are otherwise as dry as a desert.

Everyone knows that a bit of water helps crops grow, and that river mud is tip-top stuff for growing things in. But what do you do if you've got water in some places and not in others? Simple. You dig a ditch so that water flows from the watery places to the non-watery places. This way you'll turn a barren wasteland into a moist, silt-filled paradise where wheat waves golden in the breeze.

COMPLAINTS

Huge harvests have been recorded in countries such as Mesopotamia and Egypt where irrigation is commonplace.

But the people who dig the ditches are not happy with their lot.

"It's hard work," said one field hand. "We not only have to build these ditches, but we have to maintain them. You've got to clear away the silt, you've got to make sure the water runs where you want it to, and then you've got to farm the fields. And then you've probably got to dig more ditches because some bright spark has decided to irrigate the entire Arabian desert."

MASSIVE

The widespread fear is that irrigation is too difficult for farmers to do on their own, and that it will give rise to a massive workforce paid by a single, all powerful government.

"This means we'll end up with kings and stuff. They'll demand taxes to pay the workers and this will lead to a lot of hard work for us peasants," said a peasant.

TRANSPORT SPECIAL

"YOU KNOW YOU'RE GOING PLACES WITH THE SENTINEL!"

WHEEL MEET AGAIN

The Shape Of The Future

3,000 BC

It's round, it's made of wood, and it's the greatest scientific break-through since the sharp stone. Yes, it's the WHEEL!

Humans are on the road at last, and the world is rumbling to the sound of traffic as we go wheel crazy.

A potter at a wheel. Would you believe this is the first step toward the Ferrari Testarossa?

POTS

According to our reporters, the wheel was first invented by potters, who needed a round, flat thing that they could spin a lump of muddy clay on to make pot-making easier. Then one smarty-pants said, "Hey! Why not turn a couple of these on their sides, attach them to a cart, and see what happens!"

Well, the rest is history.

CANS

Nowadays, anybody who's even vaguely with-it has a set of wheels. Teenager Suzie Zagg says: "They're so cool! Because they go merrily round and round rather than drag unpleasantly along the ground, you can go places faster, and carry heavier weights than ever before!"

NUTS

Opponents are already dismissing the miracle invention as "merely an altered square." They say that although wheels allow people to move things more easily, they do have a big disadvantage: they need a smoothish surface to travel over.

Given that a lot of our terrain is made up of rocks, ravines, steep hills and impenetrable wood-land, it'll be a while before the wheel reaches its full potential.

BREATH

"Wheels are OK, but I'm not holding my breath," says mule-driver Abdullah Zupp. "In the future, whenever there's a major civilization, somebody will build roads and things will be hunky-dory.

"But when those civilizations collapse, the first thing to go is the roads... well, no roads, no wheels. Believe me, this new technology's all very clever, but the smart money's staying with pack animals."

SETTLE DOWN, SETTLE DOWN

A city. Citizens will have to wait around 5,000 years before they can complain about how bad buses are.

LIFE IS HOTTER IN SUMER!

3,000 BC

It's all change in Sumer, the Fertile Crescent's most up-and-coming region. The world's first city, Uruk, has become the biggest draw since cave painting.

"It's like a village, but much, much bigger,"

says reporter H. P. Sos. "The authorities saw how people were settling down and forming communities wherever there was enough land and water to support farming. So they decided to go one step farther. Result: the city."

Uruk really is something different. Not only is it bigger than a village, but the way it's run is entirely new. It's ruled

Here's Uruk!

by a single king who organizes citizens to dig irrigation canals, collect farm produce, police the streets and, above all, pay him taxes.

There's a big temple

in the middle of the city, which is dedicated to a god. Everybody is expected to supply the god with offerings of grain.

The king takes this grain and uses it to pay people to dig more canals, collect more farm produce, police more streets and collect more taxes so he can pay other people to defend the city, build walls around it, erect a bigger

temple, and bully the previous people into digging more canals, producing more grain and paying more taxes. (Got that straight?)

HARD

But Uruk isn't only about hardship. It's also about TRADE! The city contains lots of non-farming citizens who make their living by supplying farmers with things they don't have time to make for themselves – chairs, tables, beds, pots, jewels, garden gnomes and so on.

LONG

What this means is that, so long as you've got the grain coming in, a city will support as many trades as there is demand for them. This, in turn, means that someone can survive without farming themselves.

"Cities are the hot-bed of invention," says H. P. Sos. "I predict Uruk's example will be followed across Asia, from India to China. Once you start building these things, there's no turning back."

WRITE ON!

Clay Tablets Get Full Marks

3,000 BC

Speaking is old hat, according to citizens in Mesopotamia. They've come up with a revolutionary method of communication which involves scratching symbols on clay tablets. Enthusiasts

have already given it a name – WRITING!

"Writing's very easy," said Bart Jugg, a scribe. "All you have to do is draw a picture of the thing you want to describe. If you want to say you've got ten goats, you draw ten pictures of a goat. If you want to talk about the Sun, you draw something round with a few lines sticking out.

"After a little practice, you don't have to draw an actual goat. Instead you can do a shorthand squiggle and everybody

will recognize it as 'goat'. You can also use symbols for less obvious things. Day and night, for example. What do they look like? Easy – a sun for day and a moon for night. Some symbols are less obvious – such as an arrow, which is our sign for life. But honestly, so long as everybody knows what each symbol means, it doesn't matter what they look like. You could draw an

Is it a squiggle, or is it a WORD?

elephant as the sign for a teaspoon and that would be fine."

Royal employees are the people most likely to benefit from writing. Temple scribes will particularly welcome the development as they have to record every bit of tax paid by every man or woman in the region.

NEW THREAT TO STONE

2,500 BC

R eports are coming in of a brand new alloy called bronze. (Science fans will know that an alloy is a mixture of metals.) Developed in South-east Asia, bronze is a mixture of copper and tin. Manufacturers are hailing it as the hardest metal yet made. They have already issued a limited number of bronze weapons and expect to produce tailor-made bronze body-protection shortly.

BRONZED OFF

Supporters say the alloy marks a new era – the Bronze Age. Opponents maintain stone is still best. "If you want to avoid an arrow you don't need metal. All you have to do is duck behind the nearest rock."
The debate continues.

Metalwork – it's a dirty job, but someone's got to do it.

FOR SALE

THE EDITOR SPEAKS

The Get Ahead Sentinel – You Know It Makes Sense

Well, the Stone Age is over at last. ABOUT TIME TOO! Stone is SO unglamorous. If you want to get ahead in the world you're not going to do it by chipping away at lumps of flint. It's OK if you're starting out. But let's face it, it's not the kind of technology that's going to get us to the Moon, IS IT?

HUNTING AND GATHERING

It kept us fit, provided a varied diet and allowed us to exist in a natural state alongside the rest of the animal kingdom. But all good things come to an end. And when you think about it, it did keep population levels very low. If we'd stuck at it, most of us wouldn't be here. Since the *SENTINEL* always puts its readers first, we say that's bad news.
THE MORE OF YOU THE BETTER!!!

FIRE

Wasn't that a breakthrough? We think it'll provide the world's energy needs, in one form or another, for thousands and thousands of years. In fact, we vote it the NUMBER ONE discovery of the Stone Age!!!

MAMMOTHS

Farewell, big woolly friends. You were great while you lasted, and we shall miss your fearsome bellow. But as they say in Çatal Hüyük – this place ain't big enough for the both of us.

EVOLUTION

Whaddya reckon? WE don't think we need it any more. After all, you only evolve in order to adapt to new environments. But since we can pretty well control our environment, we don't need to adapt any more. How about THAT?!!! But there's a long way to go yet. Who knows, if they ever invent computer keyboards we might have to evolve 26 fingers.
LET'S WAIT AND SEE!

CITIES

We love 'em. Lots of buzz, lots of new ideas, lots of jobs, lots of wealthy people = lots more people reading the *SENTINEL!* THAT'S PROGRESS FOR YOU!!!

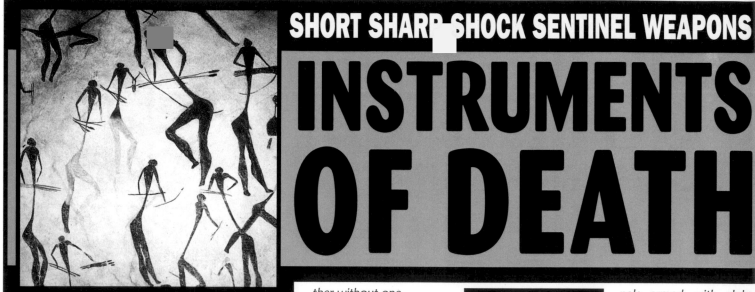

INSTRUMENTS OF DEATH

"Sticks and stones may break my bones but words will never hurt me." Anyone told they have a face like a baboon's bottom may quibble, but who could deny that sticks and stones do break bones with alarming efficiency.

Experts say that weapons are here to stay. So whether you want to kill a chicken or an attacking nomad, the choice is clear. If you're not armed, you're extinct. It's that simple.

In a special readers' service, our weapons correspondent Roy Zogg answers your killing queries.

Chomp

Dear Roy,

We're a fairly harmless bunch when you look at us. We've got dainty little fingers instead of sharp claws, and our teeth can just about chew an apple, rather than bite the head off our prey with a single chomp. We're obviously meant to be plant-munching, cuddly little creatures who like cooing at butterflies and hugging trees. So how come we're waving weapons around like there's no tomorrow?

Larry Zugg, 42 Sabre-Tooth Avenue, Hutsville

Having dainty fingers means you can make things with them. You don't see lions lashing together bows and arrows with their big nasty paws, do you? Your hand on its own can't do much as a weapon, but pick up a rock or a sharp stick and you're in business!

Two good reasons for making weapons:
*One. Try defending yourself against a pan-*ther without one.
Two. If you want to eat something more interesting than berries and seeds, chances are you'll have to catch it. True, you could hang around until you come across a half-eaten gazelle, but why wait when you can KILL IT YOURSELF!

Ferocious

Dear Roy,

This hunting is a frightening business, even if you have got a sharp stick or a flint axe! My chum Joe Gorr says it's best to hunt the biggest animals like mammoths, but I think this is too dangerous, and we should stick to killing a few dormice every now and then.

Bob Stigg, 14a Cave Crescent, Tarrpitts

Aaaaah, the great big or small debate. Face facts, Mr. Stigg. Kill a mammoth and you can keep your family fed for a month. Kill a dormouse, and you're squabbling over who gets what for breakfast, and you can forget about lunch and tea. I know mammoths can look pretty ferocious, but take it from me, they're worth the extra effort.

Worms

Dear Roy,

I'm a pretty eager hunter, with plenty of raw courage, but I'm not having much luck. Whenever I try and kill a mammoth, it runs away before I can get near it.

Jack Grok, "Dungatherin", Fossil

What you need, Mr. Grok, is TEAMWORK. Get together a bunch of pals armed with clubs and spears. No bows and arrows, or slingshots, you've got to get right up close to down a mammoth. (Tell them to get to your cave at sunrise too – the early man catcheth the mammoth.)

All huddle together in a circle. Then you say, "OK guys, what are we gonna do?" and they all shout, "Kill a mammoth!" Then you all march off into the plain going "Whoop whoop", "Yeeeahhh", and stuff like that. All the noise will rouse a sleeping

LETTER OF THE WEEK

Muuuuurdah

Dear Roy,

We all know that weapons are very good for hunting, but guess what I heard yesterday – you can even kill people with them! Quite a shock, that.

Harold Jodd, A hole in the ground, Clubland

Yes, Mr. Jodd, it's quite the latest thing. We've had weapons for ages, but until quite recently we've just used them to hunt. (Although, to be frank, there has been the odd argument over a mate or a gazelle that spilled over into a murder.)

Lately, what with fertile land getting a little scarcer now there's more of us humans around, and some of us settling down in farms and towns while others roam around, some bright sparks have realized you can kill your way to wealth and prosperity rather than work hard at it!

This is called warfare, and it basically involves all the skills we've learned from hunting – same weapons, same cooperating in groups – only the people that do it are called soldiers.

mammoth who will gal-lumph up to you to complain. This is where teamwork comes in.

While a couple of you distract its attention, the rest of you sneak around behind it. Before the mammoth can say "What's that smell", your hunting party will have it surrounded. Then you all attack at once with spears and clubs, and it's goodbye mammoth, and hello hearty mam-moth steaks! These kind of tactics work perfectly well for lions and hyenas, so they can certainly work for you too.

Homo chickiens

Dear Roy,

Yes, it's me again, Bob Stigg. It's all very well saying hunt the big stuff. I reckon you have to be crazy to want to get close enough to stick a makeshift spear into something that's fighting mad, stomping around with feet the size of cartwheels, and about the size of a five-bedroom cave.

Bob Stigg, 14a Cave Crescent, Tarrpitts

Cluck, cluck, Stigg, laid any eggs recently? But still, it takes all kinds I always say. Maybe you're good at making pots?

BASHEM & RUNN

FOR ALL YOUR SLAUGHTERING NEEDS

Still going clubbing? You're obsolete! Catch up on all the latest hi-tech weaponry, including the phenomenal no-bodily-contact bow and arrow, at a settlement showroom near you NOW!

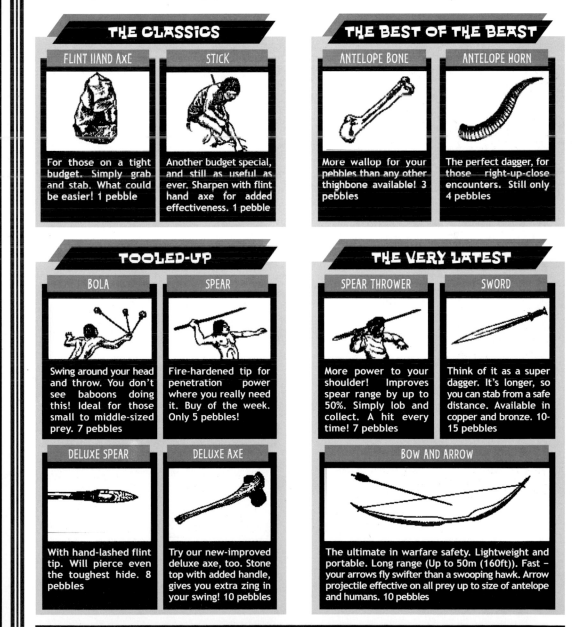

THE CLASSICS

FLINT HAND AXE

For those on a tight budget. Simply grab and stab. What could be easier! 1 pebble

STICK

Another budget special, and still as useful as ever. Sharpen with flint hand axe for added effectiveness. 1 pebble

THE BEST OF THE BEAST

ANTELOPE BONE

More wallop for your pebbles than any other thighbone available! 3 pebbles

ANTELOPE HORN

The perfect dagger, for those right-up-close encounters. Still only 4 pebbles

TOOLED-UP

BOLA

Swing around your head and throw. You don't see baboons doing this! Ideal for those small to middle-sized prey. 7 pebbles

SPEAR

Fire-hardened tip for penetration power where you really need it. Buy of the week. Only 5 pebbles!

DELUXE SPEAR

With hand-lashed flint tip. Will pierce even the toughest hide. 8 pebbles

DELUXE AXE

Try our new-improved deluxe axe, too. Stone top with added handle, gives you extra zing in your swing! 10 pebbles

THE VERY LATEST

SPEAR THROWER

More power to your shoulder! Improves spear range by up to 50%. Simply lob and collect. A hit every time! 7 pebbles

SWORD

Think of it as a super dagger. It's longer, so you can stab from a safe distance. Available in copper and bronze. 10-15 pebbles

BOW AND ARROW

The ultimate in warfare safety. Lightweight and portable. Long range (Up to 50m (160ft)). Fast – your arrows fly swifter than a swooping hawk. Arrow projectile effective on all prey up to size of antelope and humans. 10 pebbles

BASHEM AND RUNN - SLAUGHTERING SINCE 240,000BC

MRS. OGG'S STONE AGE BEAUTY PAGE

Put the stunningly sensational back into the Stone Age, with the Fashion and Beauty column you can't afford to miss!

MRS. OGG – VOTED TOP STYLE COLUMNIST OF THE ERA BY READERS OF CAVEWEAR WEEKLY

SO WHAT'S HAPPENING IN YOUR CAVE?

BEAUTY AT ITS MOST BASIC

SWAGGER

• Readers out to trap a mate will be interested to know that body painting is IN. Red clay is plentiful enough, and washes off with a simple application of water.

Other adornments to put a swagger in your stagger include ambergris perfume (this comes from whale intestines, and smells far nicer than you'd think) and spruce tree leaf resin to sweeten the breath.

You can't go wrong with a few feathers too, draped in your hair or clothing.

BEADY

• Even though they're such hard work to make, beads will always be fashionable. I know it can take up to three hours to make a single polished bead from a sliver of mammoth tusk. But once it's done, it'll stay like that forever.

A charming necklace adds allure to any outfit.

You can make beads from animal teeth, seashells, soapstone, and even pebbles. When you've got a good number, string them together to make a necklace, or sew them onto clothing using a bone needle and some wool thread.

Then you'll have something of beauty that can be passed on through the generations, and treasured by your descendants for all eternity!

HAIR WEAR NEWS

• Try braiding. This means weaving three strands into one. Not only does it keep you out of mischief, it's the perfect antidote to boring, long straight hair.

Shells make a pretty dress sensational!

FREE FACT SLAB
on clothes dyes available now!

NEXT WEEK: MAKE YOUR OWN BONE BROOCH

FASHION TIPS

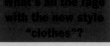
What's all the rage with the new style "clothes"?

FUR ENOUGH

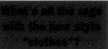

Natural materials are this season's hottest body covering, and fur is still the number one choice for Stone Age trend-setters.

It's warm, it's easy on the eye, and it doesn't take too many brain cells to realize how to wear it. It's not perfect, of course – it stinks like an old goat (especially if it IS an old goat) and it gets soggy when it rains. Still, if you want style and sophistication, you've got to pay the price!

LEATHER OR NOT

Catching up in popularity is the fabric of the future – leather. It's like fur but without the hair (you have to scrape this off.) Leather takes a while to prepare before you wear it. It has to be "tanned" (coated in a liquid called tannin to preserve it), then pulled tight across a frame to stretch it.

Leather can be cut into any shape, which means you can get it to fit as snugly as you like. You can also dye it pretty shades, or cut patterns in it.

It's extremely hard-wearing, and really keeps out the wind and the rain.

WOOL REALLY

Readers who like to peer at the very outer rim of the cutting edge of fashion technology will be curious about another new fabric. It's called wool, and it comes from those docile and bleating creatures, sheep. You can pluck it off the sheep as it sheds its coat, but don't wear it just as it is, it'll only blow off.

What you need to do is twist the wool around a wooden spindle to make a thin thread. Then you take the thread and weave it carefully together in a loom. It's very warm and versatile!

A loom. You can make socks with this!

SENTINEL LIFESTYLE SPECIAL

HAVE AN ICE DAY

THERE'S NO BUSINESS LIKE SNOW BUSINESS SAYS TOP INUIT

8,000 BC

Rudolph Reindeer's red nose would never again guide Santa through a foggy Christmas Eve.

We humans have spread to almost every inhospitable corner of the world. From the howling wastes of Siberia to the baking plains of Arizona, we're there! But how do you make a living in a land where much of the sea is frozen solid and almost the only natural resources are seals and whales and ice and snow?

"It's a piece of cake," says top Inuit Barry Yagg of the Arctic circle. "You just have to make do with the little bit of everything that's actually available." Find out how he does it with the *Sentinel*'s roving reporter Don Stigg.

Don Stigg. So what do you eat out there? I bet you get sick of seafood!

Barry Yagg. During the summer we get to eat reindeer and deer. It's winter that's mainly seafood – seal, walrus, fish – but also the odd polar bear if we can catch one. Incidentally, if you ever do catch a polar bear, don't eat the liver. It's so poisonous it'll kill you.

DS. You'll need something a bit more substantial than a hook and line to catch a seal!

BY. Too true. Sometimes we use kayak canoes and hunt with harpoons. Our kayaks are made entirely from animals – bone frame and skin covering, treated with a waterproof glue made from boiling up various animal bits and pieces.

The other way we catch sea life is by digging holes in the ice. Seals pop up in them from time to time for a breath of air, and we nab them then. (We learned this trick from our arch enemy the polar bear.)

DS. So what does the fashionable Inuit wear for a day out?

BY. From the top of our one-piece tunic and hood, to the tip of our waterproof socks and boots, all our clothes are made from animals. They're mainly the leathery hides of seals and walruses, and fur from foxes and hares. These materials keep their natural owners nice and snug, and do the trick for us too.

We like our clothes to be airtight but loose, so there's a layer of air to warm up next to our skin. We use bone needles and animal guts to sew the clothes together.

DS. Is it really true you live in ice houses?

BY. Sometimes... In the summer we're no different from everyone else. We make little huts from animal hides wrapped around a bone frame.

In the winter we also make shelters called igloos, from blocks of ice coated with snow. We have a little ice window at the top too. They make surprisingly warm little dens.

DS. There's so little wood around, what do you do for fuel?

BY. Any wood we find we use for weapons. Fortunately, our animals come to the rescue once again. The sea mammals here, such as seals and whales, are covered in a layer of thick fat called blubber, which keeps out the cold. Blubber burns very well, so we heat food with it. We also brighten up our igloos with little blubber-burning lamps!

DS. It all sounds ingenious! But honestly, why would anyone want to live somewhere where it's so freezing cold?

BY. If your idea of heaven is a beach in Majorca, then it's obviously not for you. But we like it out here – it's not too crowded, we don't have tribes of passing nomads burning our villages and stealing our corn, and if it's always cold, you soon stop complaining about it because you've never known anything else!

NEXT WEEK: SOME LIKE IT HOT – MEET THE DESERT DWELLERS!

YOU WHAT?

Get with the new-style speech in the Sentinel column that TELLS IT LIKE IT IS!

10 THINGS YOU NEVER KNEW ABOUT TALKING

1 Experts think that we hominids have been able to talk since *Homo habilis* in 2,000,000 BC, who could say a few basic words like "*food*", "*drink*" and "*do you come here often*".

2 *Homo erectus* polished up his grammar and vocabulary a bit, and was able to string together the odd sentence. "*Not… woolly… mammoth… again. Me… want… smoked… salmon.*"

3 Only *Homo sapiens* has been able to talk properly, as our mouths and throats are the right shape for rapid, sophisticated conversation. "*If I see you wearing that filthy animal skin one more time, I'm going to throw it in the fire. D'you hear? And don't look at me like that when I'm talking to you.*"

4 Humans are not the only creatures that talk to each other. Lots of animals grunt and squawk to communicate. Some insects even exchange smells to tell each other what they think. (Don't go getting any ideas…)

5 Some animals even have a small vocabulary. The Vervet monkey has about 10 different grunts and eeks, including one for eagle and one for cheetah.

6 Humans on the other hand have THOUSANDS OF WORDS for things, and can string these words together to explain complex new tricks, and let other people know exactly how they feel. (Pretty bad! Top of the world! etc, etc.)

7 These words can also describe things other people have not seen, anticipate events in the future and recall events in the past. Try doing that with a few grunts and barks.

"Errr, me think it a wolf!!!" The game of Charades swiftly follows the invention of speech.

8 To make words, your tongue goes to 50 different positions in your mouth.

9 Speech experts think it was the need to gather food together and cooperate to stay alive that led us to develop our complex languages.

10 Although words for the same thing are different all over the world, what is similar about all human speech is the basic rules of grammar. (This means the way words are arranged.)

IT'S A... CAVE

There's a word for everything these days. Tree, river, mammoth – you name it, we've got it! But where do words come from? Language eggheads have thought about this, and come up with several theories. Here at the *SENTINEL* we cast a critical eye on what they are saying...

EXPERTS SAY	THE SENTINEL SAYS
Words began as imitations of natural sounds.	Works OK for Whooosh, Splash, Burp, Woof and Meow. But how do you explain Prehistoric, Cave painting, Knife and fork... the list is endless.
Words began as utterances along with emotional reactions.	Works OK for Aaaaaagh, Bleurrrrgh and Waaaaagh, but try writing a poem with those!
Words were prompted by facial accompaniments to gestures we made to one another.	Call us crabby old cynics, but apart from a lip-smacking "Yum Yum", we can't think of anything else that fits this description.

COMMENT
THE SENTINEL SAYS

It looks like language is quite a mystery. But wherever words come from, one thing's for sure – everyone in your tribe has to use the same words to mean the same thing. After all, it's no good saying "Go and play hide and seek with a sabre-toothed tiger", if what you really mean is "Your High and Mightiness, I would be most delighted to marry your daughter."

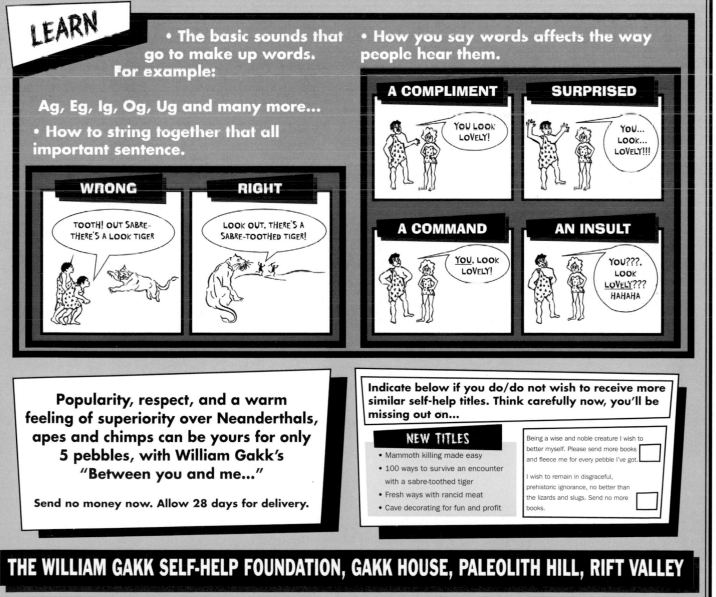

GET STUFFED

WHAT'S COOKING

with the Sentinel's cookery correspondent Pierre de Zogue

What's cooking, mes amis? Cooking is when you heat something up before you eat it!

Yes, you lazy bones, I know it takes more effort, but not only does cooked food taste, look and smell nicer, it's easier to digest and much better for you. (Nutritionists among you will be interested to know that this is because heating food makes it easier for humans to digest proteins and carbohydrates in it.)

We all know the story about the piece of mammoth meat that fell on the fire and tasted much nicer after it had sizzled a bit, but just throwing meat on a fire isn't exactly what you'd call *haute cuisine*. So what else can you do? Well, there's no end to human ingenuity…

CAKE

• If you must cook directly in a fire (and it is rather *passé* these days) try caking your meat in a juicy coating of good thick mud – it'll make it a lot more succulent, and reduces the drying up and shrinkage that direct heat often causes. Don't forget to break off the mud before you eat it!

HOLE

• Slow cooking is always better – try wrapping your meat in a big leaf and cooking on embers rather than a roaring fire.

If you're feeling really sophisticated, you can make an oven by digging a hole in the ground, filling the bottom with red-hot embers and covering up the top with a thick covering of leaves, twigs and straw. Be warned though, it can take several days to cook your food, so forward planning is called for.

PLUCK

• Another way to cook is by boiling – this means heating water until it bubbles, and then popping your food in. (Be sure to extract it with a small knife or stick. Do not, under any circumstances, pluck it from the water with your bare hands, no matter how hungry you are.)

If you're reading this before your tribe has invented cooking pots, you'll have to boil the water in a big turtle shell or reptile skin. Some enterprising chefs in Central America have even gone to the trouble of hollowing out a large stone.

SHOOT

Readers in Asia may like to clean out a thick bamboo shoot and fill that with meat, veg and a little water. Keep the bamboo far enough away from the heat to stop it catching fire, and you'll have a delicious meal. *Bon appetit*, as we like to say in this part of the world.

Hunters! Deer make a tasty dish, but people are so soppy about them. Tell your family they're eating warthog, or they may never speak to you again.

IN STYLE

FISHY STORIES

Fish make a fabulous feast and they're cheap and wholesome!

They're not the brightest sparks in the world, and anyone wanting a pet to cuddle and adore would be ill-advised to keep one, but MAKE NO MISTAKE, fish make a fabulous feast!

But how do you get hold of these silvery, slippery, succulent delicacies? FIND OUT with our infallible guide below.

BATTING

North American readers have seen Grizzly Bears do it by batting fish out of the water with their paws. Although we're quite a bit brighter than Grizzlies, for some reason we never got the hang of this.

Pierre says: Buf! Worth a go if you're desperate.

CLUBBING

You're no fool when you use a tool! Mind you, the splashing drives off any fish you haven't hit for miles around, and do watch out you don't club your own foot.

Pierre says: Alors! It's a bit crude, but then this IS the Stone Age after all.

This man knows that fish bring style and sophistication to any table.

TRAPPING

Gather up loads of sticks and laboriously lace them together to make a solid square barrier. Make several of these and then painstakingly arrange them in a V-shape reaching from the middle of the river to the bank, with a little gap at the pointy end of the V to let the fish in. Secure them to the river bed using boulders. When fish venture in, they're much easier to catch as they can't escape!

Pierre says: Zut, mes amis! This sounds harder work than killing a mammoth.

FISHING BOAT

If you're reading this before 8000 BC, when we invent the oar, you'll have to wait a while unless you're really fool-hardy. With oars we'll have a more-than-likely chance of getting back alive when we venture out to sea in little reed rafts or wooden dugout canoes.

The best way to catch fish out at sea is with a big net. You can make one of these with twisted strands of hair or twine all roped together.

Pierre says: Mon Dieu! Quite the most dangerous fishing technique available.

Sharks, whirlpools, deadly currents and tides, blistering winds and huge, huge waves await. Still, it's quite pleasant when the sun's out, and you're in with a serious chance of catching a big load of fish.

FOOD FACT HOT POT

HANDY HINTS FOR HUNGRY READERS

• Readers in the chillier parts of the world will be interested to know that meat keeps fresh much longer if you bury it in the ground. This is particularly useful if you've killed something really big, and you can't carry it all back to your cave.

• Those of you who are still hunter-gatherers may like to try digging into the ground, rather than just picking fruit and vegetables from the trees and the top soil. Readers in Europe will be interested to know that several nutritious and (fairly) digestible vegetables, such as the turnip, onion and radish can be dug up with very little effort.

American readers will be able to find potatoes and yams.

All these vegetables can be spotted by their tell-tale shoots, and they all taste much nicer after you've boiled them for 20 minutes.

• Insects make an ideal snack! Yes, it's true! Dried locusts are 75% protein and 20% fat. (That only leaves 5% grisly bits too horrible to contemplate.) So, courage, mes enfants, next time you're out on a forage and hunger strikes, munch on a moth!

FISH HOOKS

Make a hook from a horn, using a flint tool. Attach a length of string made from wool or gut. Place worm on hook. Put in river with other end of string tied to big toe. Nod off to sleep. When toe feels a twitch, pull in line – you've scored!

Pierre says: Formidable! This sounds too good to be true!

NEXT WEEK: FAST FOOD AND HOW TO CATCH IT

DAZZY DORK'S

WHAT'S HAPPENING COLUMN

SO WHO PUT THE BOMP IN THE BEAT?

Noted music profs reckon the first music happened when we discovered we could SING. Maybe we tried to imitate animal noises, maybe it was a nice hot day and we started to hum *Summertime and the living is easy* – who knows!

Then we started clapping our hands and banging sticks together, and discovered RHYTHM. Once we'd discovered that, the urge to shake our funky tail feathers and GET DOWN came upon us, and we started dancing.

Finally, we began to invent musical instruments. Maybe this started when a hunter noticed that his bowstring went THWONGGGG when he fired an arrow, and he thought, "I could write a symphony with this!"

"You put your left leg in, and your left leg out..." If <u>that's</u> what it's all about, say dancers, we'll sit this one out.

DANCE FLOOR NEWS FLASH

Movers and shakers – we all like to stamp our feet when we're strutting our funky stuff, so why not beef up that beat with an anklet of shells from the beach?

If you live inland, save yourself a trip to the seaside by stringing together rows of bones or teeth to give your dance steps that added KER-CHINKKK!

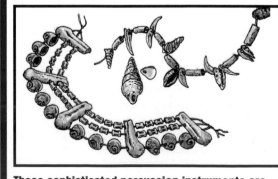

These sophisticated percussion instruments are operated by the ankle or wrist.

STONE-AGE TOP FIVE

1. Jailhouse Auroch **Elvis Zogley**

2. Where the tracks have no name **Ug2**

3. (I can't get no) huntin'-action **The Stones**

4. Eye of the (sabre-toothed) tiger **Bokk**

5. I'm a firestarter **Stigg and the Dumps**

TOOT THAT FLUTE, ZOOT

So what's hot in the world of MUSICAL INSTRUMENTS?

BUDUM BUDUM

Drummers! If you're still banging a stick on a tree, you've missed the boat maaaan! Get on the scene by stretching an animal skin over a clay pot or coconut half. You can play this with your fingers, or a stick. Alternatively, a mammoth skull makes a wonderful drum and gives a deeply satisfying K-DONK when you hit it with a heavy stick. And unlike a tree, you can take these kind of drums anywhere!

PLINK PLINK

Tight strings make all sorts of interesting sounds, but they're so QUIET. Try placing the string over the mouth of a pot as you twang it, or holding the string

next to your open mouth – you'll find it makes quite a difference to the volume (not to mention the state of your teeth.)

TOOT TOOT

Which smart alec with nothing better to do discovered you could make musical notes by blowing into a bone? Gosh, that must have been an extremely long, wet Sunday afternoon! Well you CAN, and here's how.

• Take one medium sized bird bone.
• Hollow it out.
• Add a little tube to blow into at one end.
• Make four holes along the length of the bone.

You can make different whistling noises by covering up different holes.

Be sure to tell your musician pals that this is called a flute. We'll be seeing a lot more of this kind of instrument in the future!

The flute with the tootiest toot this side of Toot House, Toot Street, Tootville!

DAZZY DORK'S NOTABLE NOTE OF THE DAY!

Hey kids! They say "music hath charms to soothe the savage beast". Personally, I'd rather face a tiger armed with a long spear than a bone flute, but, HEY, who can deny the STRANGE POWER of music!

GOOD HEALTH

with Robin Hukk, the Sentinel's medical correspondent

The column that keeps YOU up to the minute with the world of HEALTH and MEDICINE.

ILLUMINATING!

Readers often ask where illnesses come from. Most of us in the medical profession believe that minor ailments, such as runny noses, or constipation, are just part of the great ebb and flow of human existence.

However, really big ailments, like being too poorly to stand up, or being covered in lurid boils, are due to supernatural causes. Perhaps the gods are angry with you, or a malevolent demon has cast a spell on you.

Either way, if you're <u>that</u> ill, something awesome thinks you've really blotted your copy book.

FANCY A FISH SUPPER?

Nogg's Nets

For all your fishing needs

GOOD NEWS FOR SOME

Sentinel readers don't need me to tell you that it's a dangerous, unpleasant world out there. We get parched in the summer heat, and then we spend the winter shivering in our miserable tents and huts. We could get eaten by a pack of wolves one minute, or murdered by a gang of passing nomads the next.

THINGS

But don't despair, things are looking up. Thanks to recent improvements in diet, and more sophisticated weapons to protect us from predators, the average *Hom. sap. sap.* man of 10,000 BC can now expect to live for a phenomenal 30 years!

DRAWS

There's not such good news for the ladies, however. Having drawn the biological short straw of child-bearing duties, most of you can still expect a visit from the grim reaper in your mid 20s. Still, chin up, at least you don't have to go mammoth hunting!

Healthy outdoor pursuits and a good diet all mean we're living longer.

TREATMENT CORNER

Two techniques to tell you about on the treatment front. The first is for minor ailments and the second is serious do-or-die stuff.

1. Upset stomach? Nagging headache? Festering cut? "Put on those gardening gloves," say tribes who have caught on to the fact that many plants contain healing substances. You can eat them directly, or boil them up in water, or make a paste to put on a wound, the variations are endless. The

Take two of these, three times a day, with water.

64,000 pebble question is which plant for what ailment? Here at the *Sentinel* information is very sketchy, so we say "Have fun finding out!"

2. Hold tight! Medical opinion has it that the gods make people ill by putting something bad into their body like a demon or a worm, or taking something out – like the patient's soul. Treatment for these ailments consists of either putting the soul back, or casting the intruder out. In such cases, plant medicine can sometimes be effective, but more often than not, drastic methods are called for.

WHICH WITCH?

You may need to go to the expense of asking your local witchdoctor to perform a healing ceremony. (This will involve a lot of dancing and chanting, so be considerate and warn the people next door.)

WHOLE HOLE

Failing that, you could go for a trepanning. This involves having a hole drilled in your head. The advantages are that the demon or worm can then escape, or your soul can get back in. The disadvantages are extreme pain and likely death. Still, it's always worth a try if you're desperate!

THE BEGINNER'S GUIDE TO BITING THE DUST

ANOTHER READER'S SERVICE

OUR FUNERAL CORRESPONDENT DAN DED REPORTS ON THE ULTIMATE SEND-OFF

Being buried is becoming increasingly fashionable among modern day hominids. In fact, it's a sure sign that life is looking up! When you find you have time to think about what happens after you bite the dust, it means life isn't quite as nasty, brutish, and short as it used to be.

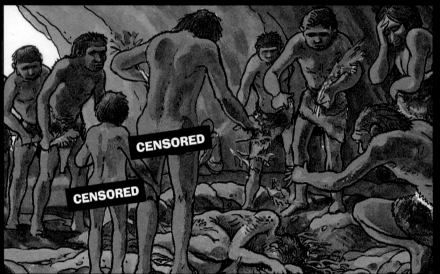

Funerals in Stone Age times are refreshingly informal, and stiff, black suits are definitely not required. It is essential, though, to bring flowers.

Testify!

Being the bright sparks we are, we've decided that we have a soul which lives on after death, and that dying is simply the moment when the soul leaves the body.

Whether you believe it goes to Heaven, the great mammoth hunting ground in the sky, or simply lurks around your tomb or cave, depends on what idea your tribe has come up with.

Vultures

In the olden days, when we were *Homo habilis* and *Homo erectus*, experts think we were so busy finding food and avoiding being eaten, we didn't make a fuss about dying at all.

If you dropped down dead, everybody else just left you there until you were eaten by a vulture. But these days we like to send our loved ones off in style, and here at the *Sentinel* we've been nosing around to see how it's done.

Neanderthal style

40,000 BC
Neanderthals were the first hominids to bury their dead, and they certainly went extinct

with a flourish!
• They dug a hole in the floor of a cave and laid the body on pine branches in a sleeping position, with its head resting on a stone pillow.
• Then they covered the body with flowers, and added some tools and a little food in case they'd be needed in the afterlife. Then they covered everything up with a nice snug layer of soil.*

Flowers will brighten up any funeral, and cost virtually nothing!

Homo Sapiens style

27,000 BC onwards
As you'd expect, *Hom. sap.* does things with a bit more sophistication.
• If you're pretty important then you're buried in some really fancy clothing – furs, hats embroidered with seashells, tunics with fox-tooth decoration, you know the sort of stuff.
• In Russia they like to bury important people with THOUSANDS of elaborately carved little

mammoth-ivory beads arranged in rows around the body.
• In France and Czechoslovakia they cover the bodies with red clay. (We think this represents blood and life.) In parts of France they also wrap the dead tightly in cloth to prevent the spirit re-entering the body and making a nuisance of itself. (Spoilsports! Here at the *Sentinel*, we think this

Funerals can be fun, so be prepared to let your hair down!

might make for an exciting evening's entertainment. After all, it'll be a while yet before anyone gets around to inventing television.)

Stones

And if you're reading this after 4,500 BC you may be interested to know that in Europe they're burying their dead in really impressive megaliths.

These are artificial caves made up of massive, heavy stones. They make an ideal shelter for a dead body or, depending on their size, a whole bunch of dead bodies.

So there, being dead doesn't have to mean being lonely. Now there's a comforting thought!

Au naturel

Finally, over in North America, *Hom. sap.* is doing things the simple way. They don't bother with anything elaborate, and rightly so. What could be easier than your so-called "Sky Burial"?

What you do is put your deceased in a high spot – up on a mountain, the top of a tree – and leave them to the weather and any passing animal who feels like a nibble.

When there's just a pile of bones left, you take these away and bury them. Ahhh, we do like to be different, don't we!?!

*Experts now disagree about the intention of Neanderthal burials. See page 10 for details.

Note to reader. Bottoms were a common sight in the Stone Ages, even at funerals. However, out of respect for the dead, we have removed them from view in our illustration.

SENTINEL SUPERNATURAL SPECIAL

STAGMAN!

WILL KURR MEETS A MAN WITH ANTLERS ON HIS HEAD

A secret camera captures Rik Vog's witchdoctor rituals for the *SENTINEL*. Hey Rik, don't put a spell on us!

et's face it. There's got to be more to existence than "Kill mammoths, then die". What's life all about? Do supernatural beings control our lives? Can we persuade the gods to look after US, rather than that tribe in the next valley who never invite us to their parties?

In this special feature, *Sentinel* religion correspondent Will Kurrr interviews a man who thinks he has the answers. It's Witchdoctor Rick Vog, of Les Trois Frères, France.

Will Kurrr: So Rik, what's with the antlers and everything?

Rick Vog: Hi, Will. This is my witchdoctor outfit. I wear it to frighten little children! Ha ha ha, just kidding. Actually, the antlers and stag mask are part of my priestly garments, along with a generous daubing of body paint.

I get dressed up like this at religious ceremonies, where all the men in our tribe gather together in a deep, dark cave. I lead them through sacred rituals to ensure that the stags and deer that we hunt will continue to live in our part of the world, and we'll never go hungry.

WK: So what do you do exactly?

RV: BIG SECRET. If I told you in detail, other tribes would copy us and they'd lure our animals away. I can tell you we do a lot of dancing and chanting, and we hand around magical objects carved out of antler and bone, and we sacrifice some animals too.

WK: So what's the point of that?

RV: It's MAGIC! You have to perform your rituals exactly right, of course. Mix up your chants, or hand around the sacred object the wrong way, and it doesn't work! I've been doing this for five years, and our tribe has never gone hungry once.

WK: So how does it work?

RV: There are lots of spirits floating around out there. They live in the most beautiful parts of the land, like waterfalls or the forest.

There are spirits in the air, and water, and earth, and fire. Some are good, some are evil. The whole point of these rituals is to keep the friendly spirits sweet with sacrifices and worship, so they'll keep you in food and good weather. If you neglect them, they leave you to the mercy of bad spirits, and that means your tribe starves because there's nothing to hunt, and everyone suffers from diseases.

WK: It sounds like a pretty important job!

RV: Too right. You can't leave anything to chance these days. We need to put a huge amount of time and effort into these ceremonies to keep us fed and healthy.

Besides which, dressing up like this is much more fun than hunting mammoths, or picking berries, but don't tell anyone in my tribe I told you!

THE SENTINEL - IT'S SPOOKILY GOOD

A SENTINEL QUIZ FOR THE WHOLE FAMILY TO ENJOY!!!

NAME THAT TOOL!

QUESTIONABLE QUESTIONS FOR THE MECHANICALLY MINDED

ANSWERS

We all know that tools have enabled us to RULE THE WORLD, and anyone worth a stuffed fieldmouse knows what an axe or a spear looks like. But what about THESE odd looking things? Guess what they are, as we ask "What on Earth is THAT?"

❶
a) A bangle?
b) A tray?
c) An early attempt at wallpaper?

❷
a) er... Is it a pastry shaper?
b) It's a saw.
c) Scrubbing brush?

❸
a) Hang on, I know this. It's for straightening spears, isn't it?
b) Is it some kind of stone pillow?
c) It's a chopstick rest.

❹
a) That's got to be a chisel.
b) No. It's a saxophone mouthpiece. I know. My brother plays one.
c) It's a fractional distillation chamber.

❺
a) Now that's a toothpick.
b) No, it's a spade.
c) You're both wrong. It's a drill.

❻
a) It's a microscope.
b) No, hang on, it's a needle!
c) You're both wrong again. It's a transmission gear connecting rod, and I know that for a FACT.

❼
a) Hmmmm. That looks like a harpoon to me.
b) Yes, I think you're right. Although it could be a back scratcher.
c) You haven't got a clue. It's OBVIOUS that it's a hat stand.

❽
a) It's a dugout canoe.
b) Naaaah, it's a toothbrush holder.
c) You're both complete cretins. Any fool can see that it's some sort of wheelbarrow.
a) I don't like your manner. Take that, punk! (CLUNK, THONK, BOP BOP BOP.)
c) Aaaaaaaaagh.

❾
a) Now that's got to be a lava hammerstone.
b) Come off it, it's just a piece of rock, anyone can see that.

---

❶ b) It's a tray made out of tree bark. You can collect berries in this.

❷ b) It's a saw. It's just right for cutting meat and grass.

❸ a) It's for straightening spears. You place your slightly bent wooden pole in it, and bend it 'til it's straight. Piece of cake!

❹ a) It's a chisel all right. You can shape antler, bone and wood with the sharp end of that.

❺ They <u>were</u> both wrong, it is a drill! You can make little holes in hide, fur, ivory, wood, in fact anything you like, with this tool.

❻ c) No, I'm just kidding, it's really b) You can make one of these with a sliver of ivory and tools 4 and 5.

❼ a) Of course it's a harpoon.

❽ a) Although the *Sentinel* in no way approves or condones any acts of gratuitous violence, we have to agree with a) that this item is most definitely a dugout canoe.

❾ b) Haha. Fooled you. It IS just a piece of rock. Incidentally, a lava hammerstone is what you use when you want to hit and shape another piece of stone.

ILLUSTRATION CREDITS

Guy Smith

and Bob Hersey, Rob McCaig, Karen Tomlins and Gerald Wood.

PHOTO CREDITS

AKG Photo, London (pages 11, 12, 23); Ancient Art and Architecture Collection, London (page 20); Robert Harding Photo Library/Rainbird, London (page 9).

This edition first published in 2016 by Usborne Publishing Ltd, Usborne House, 83-85 Saffron Hill, London EC1N 8RT, England. Copyright © Usborne Publishing Ltd, 2016, 1998.